# INTERNET SIDE HUSTLE

## YOUR NO B.S. GUIDE TO MAKING MONEY ONLINE TODAY

### BY MIKE JONES

$c\theta a$

Internet Side Hustle: Your No B.S. Guide To Making Money Online Today

Copyright © 2019 Mike Jones

First Edition, 2019

Published in the United States of America

All rights reserved. No part of this book may be reproduced or transmitted in any form or by any means, electronic or mechanical, including photocopying, recording or by any information storage and retrieval system, without written permission from the author, except for the inclusion of brief quotations in a review.

Published by COA Publishing

ISBN-13: 9781080043613

COA Publishing and the COA logo are trademarks of COA Company, LLC. Other product and company names mentioned herein may be the trademarks of their respective owners. Rather than use a trademark symbol with every occurrence of a trademarked name, we are using the names only in an editorial fashion and to the benefit of the trademark owner, with no intention of infringement of the trademark.

The information in this book is distributed on an "As Is" basis, without warranty. While every precaution has been taken in the preparation of this work, neither the author nor COA Publishing shall have any liability to any person or entity with respect to any loss or damage caused or alleged to be caused directly or indirectly by the information contained in it.

# TABLE OF CONTENTS

Introduction ..................................................................................v

Section 1: Start Making Money Today......................................... 1

Section 2: Side Hustles That Can Pay Off In A Week Or So ... 40

Section 3: Side Hustles That Require Months To Pay Off....... 57

Conclusion ................................................................................ 67

About The Author .................................................................... 69

# INTRODUCTION

This book is a summary of all my experiences and mistakes trying to make money online. Just like you, when I've heard that people can make money off the Internet, I jumped in with both feet, and just like with most other people who rushed into the online money-making game, I fell flat on my face. I needed money immediately, but I ended up doing stuff that actually requires time to generate revenue. Only after learning the ropes completely through trial and error did I figure out how everything works.

This book is the result of all my experiences and experiments. The methods that I'm going to teach you make me money every single month. I make steady money from the Internet while holding down a day job. That's right. You can keep your 9-to-5 and earn decent cash through these side hustles. What I'm going to teach you are strictly side-hustle income systems. They can be scaled up to give you a side income. This doesn't mean that you can build them up to produce a full-time income when you're ready.

## It's All about Timing

The first thing you need to know about making money online is timing. Some people need to make money immediately. Others can wait some time to incubate their online property's income generation capacity.

I've divided this book based on timeline. If you want to do something that generates cash right here, right now, I have you covered. Read the first section for that information. If you are looking for side hustles that take a longer time to generate cash, I also covered medium-term and long-term side-hustle income opportunities in this book.

Let's jump in.

# SECTION I

# Start Making Money Today

The following techniques help you earn money almost immediately. That's right. You can start making money on the side with these methods right off the bat. If you set up everything right, you don't have to wait all that long to see your first online side hustle dollar.

## Method #1: Fiverr

Fiverr is on online platform that originally allowed people to advertise their services for $5. People can buy services on this platform originally for $5. People can buy a range of services on this easy-to-use platform. Buyers can search a range of services ranging from article writing, voice-over work, graphics, you name it.

Fiverr has changed its pricing structure. Back when it started, service providers called "gig sellers" were restricted to $5. They normally could not charge than that amount. Fiverr has changed the rules so now gig sellers can pretty much charge whatever they want. Just like with any other online service platform, keep in mind that the higher your price, the fewer orders you will get. This should not be a surprise. More expensive items tend to sell at a lower rate than cheaper items. Welcome to the real world.

With that said, Fiverr is a great starting place if you want to start making online income on the side.

## How to Use Fiverr

Fiverr helps people looking for a side hustle sell their services. It is primarily a service sales platform. Keep this in mind. For the most part, you're going to be selling your time. When you sell a service, people ask you to do a custom job so you take the time to do the job and then you upload your digital work product. Maybe it's a Word document, perhaps it's a graphics file, or it can be a report of documenting online promotions work you did for the client. Whatever form it takes, you have to upload all materials to Fiverr.

This platform bans people for trying to get in direct contact with their clients. You cannot contact people through their e-mail addresses. You have to do all your communications through the platform. This is one restriction that many freelancers don't like about Fiverr.

Unless you're willing to break the rules and post your e-mail address, it's usually not advisable. Fiverr does a great job of delivering clients, but if they catch you, it's going to be very hard for you to get new clients, they will probably ban you. Your order's flow will dry up quickly. It's always a good idea to play by the rules.

## Step #1: Pick a service you can do quickly.

Since you're going to be trading your time for money you have to make sure you pick a service that you can do quickly. Now this assumes that you can provide a service in the first place. To find out, look through the different categories available on the site. You can try article writing, video work, graphics, it doesn't really matter. Just go through the different categories as well as sub-listings and see which of these you can already do.

You have to understand if you want to make money off Fiverr, you have to offer a service that you can do right here, right now. Don't offer something that you're still learning to do because you are going to be rated partially by delivery time. The sooner you can deliver, the better. This increases the chances that people will come back to you to order your services again and again.

If you take a long time to deliver, or if your work quality sucks don't expect repeat business. In fact, don't expect much business at all because every negative review and rating you get from the site will reduce your gig visibility on that platform.

## Step #2: Pay attention to category popularity

At this point, you should have a clear idea of the services that you can do based on your browsing of Fiverr. You've gone through the many different gigs on offer. You compared them with your skill set. You should have a fairly good idea of what kind of service you can offer on Fiverr. In fact, you might be quite excited at this point.

Don't jump in just yet. Pay attention to the number of gigs per category. If you notice that certain categories have a lot more gigs than others, this indicates that there is a tremendous demand for that type of service. Make a list of all the services that you're skilled enough to do. Go through different categories based on the number of gigs in each category. Delete items on your list that are in categories that don't have that many gigs. Hang on to the gigs that arc in fairly popular categories.

## Step #3: Size up your work.

Now that you have a list of categories that are in good demand, which line up with your skill set, you need to look at the gigs for sale on in those categories. Look at the samples offered by gig sellers. Can you come up with something comparable? Can your work quality match their output?

If not, you might want to scratch off that category from your list. You need to pick service categories that you excel in. Your work quality must meet or beat the existing quality offered by the service providers.

## Step #4: Pick services you can deliver on time.

Your next step is to look at the remaining gigs on your list and note the average turnaround time. This is very important because you're going to be trading your time for money. You have to get a good idea of the average turnaround time.

Once you have this, do a test. Try to perform the work for the remaining gig services on your list and see if you can deliver these on time. If you can't, scratch them off your list.

## Step #5: Pick gigs with decent ROI.

You're the only person who knows what your time is worth. With that said, I suggest you look at your 9-to-5 job and figure out your hourly rate. Next, figure out how long it would take for you to produce the work for the gigs you're thinking of offering. This should be the target price for your gig.

For example, if you work as an accountant and your hourly rate is $50 per hour but you can live with a $25 side hustle, see if you can complete the test gig within 1 hour. If it takes you two hours, then your target price for your gig should be $50. After all, it takes you two hours.

Next, check out all the gigs that are similar to the service you want to offer and look at their price. Do they come close to the price you'd like to charge? If you notice that these services cost way below your target price, you might want to scratch off that service from your shortlist. It won't meet your ROI.

You need to be completely honest with yourself here. A lot of people looking for side hustles would take a steep discount. Their 9-to-5 pay $50 per hour but they can go down to $10 an hour. Just make sure you multiply the hourly rate you can live with, with the comfortable estimated amount of time it takes you to produce the product your potential clients will order.

## Step #6: Pick your gigs.

At this point, you should have selected the one, two or handful of gigs you will be offering. Again, these have to make economic sense for you to offer. Don't paint yourself in a corner where you are going to be making very, very low money per hour, just because you want to sell your spare time. Pricing yourself that low will not be sustainable. Chances are you probably will quit Fiverr sooner than you would like because you did that. Make sure you are comfortable with the price that you're going to be charging.

## Step #7: Create an ad for each service.

Winning ads on Fiverr share certain common features. Make sure you do the following:

Use Keywords in Your Title

If you notice that certain keywords in your competitor's ads show up all the time, use that keyword. Write a gig description like a resume. Effective resumes are written in a very active voice. Make sure you do the same with your ad.

Get the reader excited about ordering your service. Focus on the benefits they will get. I am not talking about just saving money. I'm talking about how it would take their business or their personal lives to the next level. Think in terms of the needs of your potential customers and speak to those needs.

If you're offering graphics, describe your graphic service in terms of how many sales it can produce or how much clearer content featuring those graphics will appear to blog readers. Focus on benefits to the end-user, not just your client.

Next, you should offer several samples of your work. The more samples you post up, the better. When you browse through Fiverr, you will quickly notice that a lot of your competitors only have one or a couple of samples with their gigs. In fact, a lot of service providers don't even have samples. The more samples you show with your service, the more you will stick out.

Feature a video. You should create a video slideshow of your creation process, maybe you should shoot a video of yourself telling the reader what they could expect from your work. However you want to do it, make sure it's personal. It has to feature you, what you think about your work, your production philosophy, so people can get the impression that they are building a relationship with you.

Please remember that a lot of people who buy from Fiverr are not one-time buyers. The bulk of Fiverr's annual sales are actually generated by repeat buyers. These are people who buy dozens if not hundreds of times every single year.

Appeal to those people. Try to make a personal connection with them. Give them the impression that they can trust you for the long haul. Make it clear to your prospects that you are not just looking for a one-shot deal. You're not just looking to do a job for them one time. Instead, position yourself as their potential "go-to" source for all their needs regarding a particular type of service. The best way to get this message across, of course, is through video.

## Step #8: Promote your gig.

The problem with Fiverr and other seller-based freelancing platforms is that you're caught in a chicken-or-egg problem. People won't buy from you because you don't have existing clients. You can't get clients because people won't buy from you. It's a Catch-22.

To break from this, you can do one of two things. A lot of sellers on Fiverr just simply wait. They just hope that somebody will take a risk on them and they do a good job. These people come back for more and, soon enough, as the service provider gets more and more reviews, their gig's visibility rises on Fiverr, and they get a lot more organic traffic.

This sounds awesome and everything, but it definitely takes time. It also takes a lot of luck. If you are in a very competitive category, this probably will not happen. Moreover, if you are offering a service that doesn't have much demand, this scenario probably will not take place. Either that or it will take a longer time.

The alternative is, of course, to spread the word about your Fiverr gig to your friends and family. Ask or even beg them to buy your service. The more they create accounts and buy your purchase, the more reviews you get. Since these are your friends and family members, chances are they will give you the best ratings and glowing reviews. The more they build you up, the higher the chance you will start organically pulling in buyers from Fiverr. You're reaching out to people you know so you can jump-start your gig. Either way, you speed up the process. You might still get there organically, but be prepared to wait.

When I was first started out on Fiverr, I was off to a fairly slow start. It took several weeks for me to get more than two orders per week, but once I started getting a steady stream of buyers, people were buying pretty much daily. I made several thousand dollars on Fiverr over a year. It can be done.

However, if you want to turbo-charge your side-hustle income from Fiverr, you might want to be more proactive and spread the word about your gig to your family members, coworkers and other people who you think would want to help you out.

## Gig Ideas

I know I told you to look at the different gigs available at categories and size them up with your skills. I also told you to come up with test samples of work product and see if they match the quality of the stuff being offered on Fiverr. If you are stumped or you don't know where to start or just want some ready suggestions for gigs you can offer, check out the listings and descriptions below.

Please note that I have separated the gig types into two categories: active work and passive work. Active work is exactly that. You're selling your time. When somebody places an order, you do the work, you send them the result and then you get paid. No order, no work.

Passive work, in my opinion, is better. You do the work once, and when somebody orders, you send them a copy of your work. When another person orders, you go to your hard drive, open a folder and upload another copy of that work. You can repeat this over and over again. You don't have to work for each new order. That's why it's passive income.

In my opinion, this is the best way to earn side-hustle income. However, on Fiverr there are only limited opportunities to do this. I'll describe those gigs later on.

# Active-Work Gigs

## Write for Others

There are tons of bloggers, article marketers, online store owners and other digital publishers who use Fiverr to get original content. For a variety reasons, they cannot write their own stuff. Maybe their English isn't very good. Perhaps they just don't have the time. Possibly, they just don't have the time. They're probably not all that confident about their text. Whatever the reason is they turn to Fiverr to look for articles, blog posts, product reviews and other written work.

If you know how to write well enough, you might want to consider writing for others. Keep in mind that the amount of time you spend writing also includes research time. Always factor in research time. This is where a lot of would-be Fiverr writers slip up. They automatically assume that the time they spend producing content is just writing. Well, anybody can write.

If you're a fast-enough typist, you can theoretically make a lot of money on Fiverr. However, the problem is if you factor in your research time, this can cut your income. Always keep research time in mind when deciding your price.

## Social Media Commenting

Believe it or not when people comment on YouTube, Facebook or even Twitter, customers will pay for that service. It's easy to why they would do that because people looking to buy products, pay attention to reviews or semi-reviews posted on comments. Other people also look for information written in the comment section, which can promote some sort of article.

## You Can Also Sell Blog Commenting Services

Another common gig at Fiverr involves service providers leaving comments on clients' blogs or third party blogs. Traditionally, this service fell under search engine optimization. The idea was to comment on a blog and use target keywords as the "name" of the commenter, and link these keywords to the website being optimized for search engines.

Thanks to Google Penguin and Google's long running warpath against link spamming, this practice has gone away. Very few legitimate SEOs build links this way.

So why do people still offer manual commenting services on blogs on Fiverr? Believe it or not, when people read blog posts, they often check the comments section. Maybe there's a piece of information that's missing from the post. Maybe the post opened certain issues that would be discussed further in the comments. Whatever the case may be, a significant portion of blog post readers read the comments. This poses a tremendous marketing opportunity.

Customers looking for this blog commenting service recognize this opportunity. The key here is to come up with "natural" and interesting comments that actually adds value to the blog post.

This is not always easy. You really have to know your stuff. You can't just drop a link and call it a day. It doesn't work that way. If you do that, not only will your comment get deleted, but your customer probably would want a refund.

Think of manual blog comments as a step down from formal blog post or article writing. It really is a form of writing because you have to contribute some sort of value for people to actually want to read your comment and take it seriously. Until and unless you do that would they then take the next step of clicking on a link or, better yet, do a search for a concept you introduced in your blog comments.

Believe it or not, this type of service can be quite lucrative. Highly effective blog commenters are few and far between. These people really know their stuff because they not only know how to attract attention, but they draw a tight fit between what the reader would be interested in and what their clients are promoting.

## Translation Gigs

If you know a foreign language, you might want to sell translation services on Fiverr. Now, please understand that while Fiverr does have a global marketplace, there is a hierarchy of languages in terms of market demand. While the top five languages do fluctuate over time, Mandarin Chinese, Spanish and French usually are in the top five. If you know these languages, you might want to sell translation services.

Now, please understand that you have to have great grammar. You also have to have a good command of idioms. You can't just pull random translations of words from one language to another because context means a lot.

Native speakers of the language you're translating can easily detect context. And if you pick the wrong words, your client is going to look like a fool. How happy do you think they would be if their intended audiences laugh at them or fail to take them seriously?

Please understand that highly effective translations don't just mean taking words from one language and translating it to another language on a wholesale basis. You have to also pay attention to context and also use the right words to convey the meaning your client is trying to get across. This is not exactly easy.

## Sell Your Expertise in the Form of Advice

Believe it or not, regardless of your background, you're probably an expert in something. Maybe you're good with cars, maybe you know how to bake a muffin, maybe you have been to Hong Kong, Thailand, Taiwan, China and you can advise people who are thinking of visiting there. Whatever your experience is, you can bet that somebody would want your advice.

I've seen people on Fiverr offering decision-making services. That's right. You just need to send them the facts of your issue, and they will make a decision for you.

This highlights the fact that regardless of where you come from, what you've been through, or what your educational attainment is, you have some sort of expertise. The best way to know this is to just post it up on Fiverr and see if somebody orders it.

Of course, certain types of advice are in higher demand. For example, business decisions tend to be in higher demand than advice regarding video games. You get my point. You should just post up all sorts of advice and services and see which ones get traction.

## Compose Music on Demand

Another service you can offer on Fiverr involves music composition. You can compose original music or scores for customers. It's important that you have the right equipment and software to do this.

People order this service because they're looking for royalty-free music. Whatever stock music is available to them simply isn't cutting it, that's why they come to you. To sell well in this space, you have to post a lot of samples, and they better sound good.

Also, you should focus on a niche. For example, if you play a lot of video games and you know certain scenarios in video games and have creative ideas on music that would sound well, come up with such music and explain that this would make for great video game music in certain settings. The more niches you cover and the more specialized those niches, the higher the chance you would sell. This also increases the chance that people will pay you a decent amount of money for original music.

Niche specialization is important, although you can also play the game the other way. You can also approach this from the other side. You can come up with fairly generic music, which you can then sell many times over in the form of PLR audio files. I'll discuss that approach in the passive income portion of this book.

## Sell Handicrafts

If you like to do scrapbooking or you do arts and crafts at home, you can sell physical goods via Fiverr. Fiverr will basically act as your marketing platform to sell stuff that you create on your spare time.

The big challenge here is to find crafts that are in high enough demand. While I'm sure that there is at least one person out there that would love to pay good money for custom crafted coca cola cans, the demand for that is fairly limited.

So to maximize your return on effort, you might want to look through the different crafts listings on Fiverr and zero in on the most popular craft areas. See if you can create better products than those on offer.

To cross reference your estimates, look at Etsy and Pinterest. The more pictures on Pinterest involving your particular arts and crafts niche, the higher the chance that there's a robust demand for it. The same applies to Etsy. The key here is to not waste your time creating crafts that nobody wants.

## Distribute Flyers on Demand

Another service you can provide involves flyer distribution. This is quite popular on Fiverr.

The downside is that you have to live in the part of the United States that has a fairly big population. This is very important. It has to be densely populated enough for your prospective customers to demand flyer distribution there. Usually, these gigs involve 25 up to 50 flyers at a time.

You also have to offer some sort of documentation. Maybe you should take pictures or videos of you handing out the flyers. Another way to document the effectiveness of your flyer distribution campaign involves the response URL or response phone number or code included in the text of the flyer itself.

## Promote at Famous Landmarks

Another common service on Fiverr involves gig sellers holding up a sign or wearing special clothing on famous landmarks. I've seen a person hold up custom signs at the Brandenburg Gate in Berlin, Germany. Other people would hold up signs in other famous places.

There's quite a bit of demand for this because it's actually the landmark that the clients are interested in. The idea is, when people see the Eiffel Tower in the background and the name of their company, there is some sort of interest there. It becomes very interesting to a lot of people because, usually, people recognize the landmark, and if you tie that in with some sort of local brand, you draw attention to the brand. Well, at least that's the theory. Regardless, there's quite a bit of a demand here.

Of course, the obvious drawback is that you have to live near a famous enough landmark. This is not always the case. If you live in many parts of the United States, there may be landmarks in your state, but they're far away. Also, they might not be as well-known as the Golden Gate Bridge or the Statue of Liberty or Mount Rushmore. This might be a limited opportunity for you.

Another thing that you need to keep in mind is your cost of getting from where you live to the landmark. Now, this is great if you live in New York and you can easily walk to the Statue of Liberty. This is going to be a problem if you live very far from the

Grand Canyon in Arizona and you'd have to jump into your car and burn some gas to get to that landmark.

## Passive Work on Fiverr

When it comes to side hustles, passive work excites me more than active work. It truly does. While I love to work for every dollar I earn, it gets old quickly. Seriously.

When you are doing active work, you are trading in your time for money. Whether you are holding up a sign at a famous landmark, handing out flyers, selling your crafts, writing custom music, giving out custom advice, doing on demand translations or doing a wide variety of writing, you burn up a lot of time.

And unfortunately, you cannot recycle that time. Whatever work product you produce with that time is the property of your client. This is called "work for hire." All intellectual property rights go to your client.

What if I told you that you can work once to create a product, but you get to sell that product many times over? In other words, you recycle your time. You're not trading in time for dollars. Instead, you did the work once, you put in the time once, and then it continues to pull in dollars over an extended period of time. This is called passive income.

Thankfully, the internet has made this so easy. On Fiverr, there are several passive income opportunities that you should look into.

On a dollar per dollar and minute per minute basis, I prefer passive work to generating a side hustle. I just need to sign on to Fiverr, check out my orders, and then go through my computer's subfolders to upload copies of work I did in the past. Once I've done that, I generate a few hundred bucks, and I call it a day.

This beats having to sit down, read the instructions of the client, write out an article or do commenting or do any kind of custom work and make sure that you don't take too much time. If you blow your time limit, you're actually losing money providing that service. It doesn't even compare.

So do yourself a big favor, if you can, and try to generate passive income from Fiverr instead of active work. Chances are, you probably need to do active work first to get used to how this works, and then start offering pre-made content.

Here are just some ideas. You can actually come up with many more ideas. These are just intended to inspire you to get you to brainstorm.

## Sell Canned Advice

Let's face it, a lot of people are lazy. When it comes to getting advice, you can pretty much get 90% of all the information you need by simply doing Google searches. That's the bottom line. If you're not lazy, you can use Google to find pretty much 90% of the information you're looking for.

But the problem is, either people are lazy, they're not all that smart, or they don't have the time. Whatever the case may be with your clients, they're looking to pay for advice. Wouldn't it be awesome for you to write an advice once, and then sell it many times over?

This is exactly what you do when you're selling canned advice. It's already an existing package, and you're just distributing it through Fiverr. The secret to this, of course, is niche. You need to find advice that people constantly ask for. There has to be a tremendous demand for this type of advice.

How exactly do you determine demand? Do searches on Google. If you notice that the same question keeps popping up, chances are, a lot of people are interested in that question.

Go to places like Quora. This is a question and answer platform. Look at how many times that same question has been asked. Pay attention to how many people follow those questions. This should give you a fairly good idea of just how popular certain advice categories are.

You should come up with advice that is very detailed and covers as many different sub-issues or sub-questions in your target niche.

I would suggest that you promote your passive products using your active gig ads on Fiverr. This way, when people look at your active services, they can see that there's an option for a canned solution. Obviously, you should sell the canned advice at a lower rate to motivate people to click on the passive product's link.

## Sell Your Pre-made Crafts Plans

If you are big into handicrafts, you know that these are hard to do from scratch. People need some sort of template. They need some sort of plan to work from. These materials make for great passive sources of income. You can just send a PDF file to people looking to make some crafts along with instructions. Again, you have to size up the demand for these plans.

Please remember that many people are lazy. They don't want to learn how to do arts and crafts. They just want to buy the finished product. However, if you notice through your research online that a lot of people are asking questions on how to do this using some sort of list or some sort of instructional video, then you might want to sell your plans, templates, or patterns.

## Sell Flyer Templates

If you are a very creative person and you make flyers that attract a lot of attention, you might want to sell the templates for those flyers. Local businesses are always looking for flyer ideas. The key here is to identify niches that people are most interested in.

For example, maybe you would come up with a pizza shop flyer. Obviously, pizza restaurants would buy that flyer template.

The same goes with real estate. Look at typical suburbs and towns in the United States and see their business type distribution. Use that as a guide to help you create different templates for those types of businesses.

Of course, the more diverse your range of flyer templates are, the higher the likelihood people would order your templates. It also would help if you would include instructions on how to modify the templates as well as limitations on what they can put into the file and ensure it still looks good.

## Sell Email Swipe Files

Let me tell you, writing effective email is an art form. There are no two ways about it. You can't just take a random person and ask that person to come up with highly effective emails. It's just not going to happen.

People who make money through their email lists have gone through the process of figuring out headlines that get opened as well as email bodies that catch people's attention. This takes a lot of work and experience. People know this. This is why they pay top dollars for email writers.

However, there are online entrepreneurs who don't have the budget for that, but still need high quality email files. This is where you come in. You can identify certain hot niches and then create pre-packaged email swipe files to cater to those niches.

Just like with other market research I mentioned in this book, you need to do niche research. Focus on what's already selling.

## Sell Research

If you've ever written articles, you know that it can be a headache doing research. Wouldn't it be nice if you had some sort of cheat sheet that you can easily refer to so you can just lift important information that would make your articles more authoritative and credible?

Believe me, there's quite a bit of a demand for this. You can sell research cheat sheets targeting certain industries. What makes this tricky is that you need to find the right niche. Again, follow my advice on niche research so you know which research niches to focus on.

## Audio Gigs

What follows are some services that you can offer if you have access to a high quality microphone. On Fiverr, a lot of buyers are interested in voice-over or narration work. Some are looking for professional quality voice-overs, others are looking for a more natural sounding voice work. Keep this in mind.

If you're going to be selling voice work, make sure you position your service accurately. If your voice and pronunciation is not all that professional, let your prospective client know. Don't mislead them. Don't pass yourself off as somebody you're not. Regardless of how you do it, make sure you include several samples of your voice in your gig page so the prospective buyer knows exactly what he or she is getting into.

## Narration Gigs

Narration gigs simply involve you reading pre-prepared text. You just have to read the text in an engaging way. You can't sound like somebody who's bored. You can't read the materials in a way that puts the listener to sleep. If you're able to do that, then you should be able to get some orders as a narrator.

Now, to get a competitive advantage, you need to narrate more words than your competitors. Sure, they may have better voices than you, they may even have professional experience, but if you are going to be reading more words, you'd be surprised as to how popular your gig can be.

A lot of the people looking to buy narration services on Fiverr are looking for a good deal. They know that highly professional narrators charge $10 for 50 words or less. That's too little.

If you were to charge $10 for 200 words, you're going to stand out. The longer the narration, the more competitive your price, the higher the chance you will get a lot of customers. A lot of these will probably keep coming back.

## Offer Voice-Overs

If you have a very entertaining voice and you can pack quite a bit of emotion in what you say, you can make quite a bit of money selling voice-overs.

Now, with that said, please understand that this is very competitive because people are looking for high quality. You want people to get excited over your voice. You want people to notice the value of the offer you are discussing. You might have to do several takes to get the right message across. This is why you need to price your voice-over work wisely.

It's very tempting to just offer this for $5, but let me tell you, highly effective voice-over work involves several takes. You might have to record several times to get it just right. That $5 you're charging starts becoming really, really cheap and unprofitable with each take.

Do yourself a big favor and offer voice-over work only after you have practiced extensively. Don't just jump in with both feet and offer voice-over work because you'll get blown away by the competition. What's worse, when people start posting negative reviews of your work, that's pretty much game over for you.

## Video Gigs

Another category of gigs you can offer on Fiverr involves videos. If you just have a webcam on your computer, that equipment is good enough.

You can offer all sorts of videos. You can do testimonials after reading a client's book, or you can take a video of yourself getting all excited about a product that they are launching.

Of course, a lot of these testimonials are fake, so there may be legality issues. You might want to check the terms and conditions of Fiverr to see the legal limits of testimonial videos.

Maybe the way to get around this would be for you to dramatize reasons why people would want to be interested in the product the client is offering.

Review Websites

Another popular category of testimonial videos on Fiverr involves reviews of websites. When people check out a site, they have all sorts of impressions. You can share this information on a video. There are quite a number of clients who would be interested in such videos.

## Sell "How To" Video Gigs

These "how to" videos involve people talking about how to do certain things. They are often overlays of bullet points and steps they need to take. Of course, the more special effects are involved, the more you charge for the video.

Please understand that most of the time, you are the star of the show, so your face will show. Keep this in mind. Some people are quite shy when it comes to showing their face for instructional videos.

## Slideshows

This is my personal favorite. The great thing about slideshows is that you don't necessarily have to show your face. You also don't have to feature your voice. You can just show slides with text and intersperse them with actual video clips.

You can use slideshow generation software to create MP4 files that your clients can upload to places like YouTube.

This type of service is very popular. It's also not all that hard to do. You have to have a script. Also, you can get your client to supply you with all the images and you just put them all together to produce the slideshow.

Of course, this can take quite a bit of time if you're just starting out, so make sure the price you charge accurately reflects the amount of time you will be spending creating these slideshow videos.

## More Passive Income Ideas for Fiverr

Again, the great thing about passive income is that you work once, but you sell your work product many times over. You work to get the product done, and then you use Fiverr to sell this product many times.

Generally, people charge $5 for these items, but depending on demand for the item as well as the quality of your work, you can actually charge more than $5. It really all boils down to the level of demand and how specialized the product is.

## Sell Fiverr Books

Sell books that help people find services on Fiverr or anything related to the services that they find on Fiverr.

I know this sounds crazy, but a lot of people are stumped on how to use Fiverr properly. In fact, a lot of people use Fiverr in a very shallow way. They just look for one type of service, and they're really clueless as to the wide range of benefits they can get from that platform.

You can sell a fairly short PDF book on Fiverr teaching people to make full use of this site. This means you have to research Fiverr intensively, get your notes down, write the book, and then find a way to promote it to people who use Fiverr regularly.

## Sell Contacts Research

This is one of my personal passive income favorites. The great thing about LinkedIn is that it segregates people by industry. This is all self-reported, mind you. People actually would tell LinkedIn what kind of industry they're in. There are even sub-industries that they include in their profile.

If you know your way around LinkedIn, you can grab contact information from people's profiles and create reports by niche. For example, you can create a report on personal injury lawyers in Los Angeles. You can also get together a report on plastic surgeons in Las Vegas. The possibilities are endless.

You then sell these packages on Fiverr. It's important that the contact information must be publicly available. This way, you don't get sued. Also, you have to sell contacts in industries that have a high demand.

For example, structured settlement companies are only in demand with lawyers or certain types of plaintiffs. You're probably not going to be selling much of those. Look for the types of professional contacts that people are eagerly looking for, so there's a high chance that you would actually make a good passive income from that canned research.

To save money, you might want to hire a virtual assistant from places with lots of people who speak English as a second language. I am, of course, talking about places like India, Bangladesh, Kenya, the Philippines, and Pakistan. You can get your virtual assistant to compile all this information once, you can edit it and format it, and then sell the custom research on Fiverr and other platforms.

## Sell Stock Photos

If you're a photographer or you have legal access as well as rights to resell somebody else's photo work, you might want to sell stock photos. This is a tremendous market because people looking to post any kind of material online are looking to capture the essence of the content that they produce.

Unfortunately, when you go to a regular stock photo site or a free photo site, a lot of those photos look too familiar. Maybe they don't properly capture the essence of the article or post. Whatever the case may be, they don't fit.

A lot of publishers are turning to Fiverr to look for canned photos that may do a better job representing the mood or sentiment of their article or blog post.

## You can Always Sell PLR Books

PLR or private label rights is an intellectual property legal concept that enables content creators to sell the rights to use such content to buyers. When people buy your PLR book, they're essentially getting a license to sell the book or present the book as their own work. Now, you can go quite far with PLR rights, but that's the essential gist of it.

There's still quite a bit of demand for PLR books because, for a wide variety of reasons, a lot of people find it hard to write their own custom books. It definitely costs a lot more money and takes quite a bit of time.

The secret to selling a lot of PLR books boils down to niche research. You need to sell PLR books that are in high enough demand.

To do this, you have to do extensive analysis of the PLR items on sale on Fiverr. Make sure that you're not selling the exact same stuff that everybody else is selling. That's just not going to work. At the same time, you're going to have to also find items that are in high enough demand.

How can you determine demand? Well, one way to do this is to use Google AdWords' keyword planner tool. This tool will help you find keywords related to the niche of the books you're trying to write and see how often people search for those keywords in the space of a month. This should give you a fairly rough idea of overall demand.

Also, you might want to type in related keywords into Google to determine how many sites target such keywords. This shows you how competitive the space is. Obviously, people would not be making all these websites if there was no demand.

By comparing these two data sets together, you should have a fairly rough idea of the demand for certain niches. Use this information to guide you in picking the niches for your book.

# Money Making Method #2: Other Freelance Websites

Make no mistake about it, Fiverr is a freelancing platform. However, this platform requires freelancers to offer their services, and buyers look through the service descriptions when deciding to buy.

Other freelance platforms have it in reverse. Places like Upwork and Freelancer.com feature the job order of the client. The freelancers would then send their bids or applications for the freelance job on offer.

Other places you can look involve marketing sites. Sites like Warrior Forum and Black Hat World have areas where members looking to hire freelancers would post their job descriptions. You go to these sections and look for their contact information to get in touch with them about their project.

Finally, you can also post your service ad on the job sections of these marketing forums. However, not all marketing forums have jobs, classifieds or marketplace sections. Still, if you find these, you might want to consider posting an ad.

## Success Tips with Freelance Sites

Now that you have a clear idea of how freelance websites and platforms work, here are some tips that may increase your chances of getting more customers.

## Personalize Your Profile

When creating a profile, you shouldn't just go through the motions. You shouldn't look at this as a simple form-filling or data entry. You have to use all aspects of the form to make you look distinctive. You have to attract attention. You have to get people to see what's different about you.

You have to understand that the problem with too many freelance platforms is that there are tons of people bidding for the same job. And a lot of these people just filled out their profile. They don't look different from each other. They didn't include samples, and they wrote their profiles in a very boring way. Not surprisingly, most of them don't get noticed. It's as if they fall between the cracks.

You have to personalize your profile. You have to grab the potential client's eyeballs and slap it a couple of times to let the person know that you're different. You bring something significant to the table.

## Always Include Work Samples

One of the main reasons why a lot of freelancers on a wide range of freelance platforms fail is the fact that they're too lazy. They simply did not go through the process of finding their best work samples and posting it online.

You have to understand that when people are looking to hire a contractor, they want to be reassured. They are scared stiff of the possibility that they might hire the wrong person. That's where they're coming from.

Set their minds at ease by showing them a wide range of work samples. The more samples you can post, the better. This lets the person know that you have done a wide range of jobs related to the kind of task they're looking for. This demonstrates, in no uncertain terms, that you are an experienced person. At the very least, you know how to produce work output.

There is a certain level of predictability there. Since they can see your portfolio, they have a certain level of assurance that the quality that you would produce for them will not be all that far off. Always include work samples. This is non-negotiable.

If you are too lazy to post up work samples, you might as well not do this. Seriously. You're not going to get that many jobs. People are not going to gamble on you. Nine times out of ten, when two applicants step up, with one having a portfolio and the other simply saying "trust me," the prospective client will go with the contractor with the sample.

## Write Your Profile Like a Resume

If you have done your fair share of resume writing, you know that you have to engage the reader. When a person's reading through your experience, they can see themselves witnessing you doing certain work. Not only that, they can see that the things that you did were crucial for the organizations that you work for. At the very least, they can see the value you bring to the table.

Use that same writing style to write your profile. You want prospective clients to get excited about hiring you. You want them to be clear on the kind of value they can expect from you.

## Reverse Engineer Other Freelancers' Profiles

If you're having a tough time coming up with your own profile, do yourself a big favor, look for successful freelancers that offer the same service as you.

On freelancing sites like Upwork, there are certain indications of past success. Look for the most successful freelancers that offer roughly the same service as you. Pay attention to what their profiles say. What do they all have in common? How are they written? What do their samples look like?

Once you have this information, come up with your own version. Reverse engineer their profiles. Make them do your homework.

This way, you get a head start. You're not starting from scratch. You're not doing some sort of wild guess, and you're not taking shots in the dark. You are using their existing profile. And you know from their past success that somehow, some way, their profiles work.

## Always Send Custom PM

When bidding for projects, do yourself a big favor and reach out to the prospective clients. You may think that this may be annoying, but it actually counts for a lot.

A lot of bidders would simply make a bid and go away. They're essentially just rolling the dice and hoping that somehow, some way, they get picked. If you take the extra step of sending a custom message to the client asking either for more information or somehow communicating your desire to know more about their project, you stand out from the crowd.

Now, this might not necessarily mean that you would get the job, but at the very least, you look more distinctive. Often times, that's all it takes because a lot of the times, these clients are in a hurry. They need to make a decision now. If you stand out asking these questions, they are more likely to look at your portfolio and check out what you are about. That may be the competitive edge that you need to land that job.

## Customize Your Offer

Another common mistake freelancers make is that they use some sort of template to make bids on jobs. They say the same stuff over and over again.

Nine times out of ten, your offer is probably not going to get read. Seriously. Why? Since you're using a template, you're not really speaking to a wide range of needs and concerns that are specific to that particular job order. You might come off like somebody who is clueless regarding a very important detail.

When you customize your offers and mention certain details from the job order, this communicates three things to your prospective client. First, they notice that you actually read their ad. They feel special because they now know that you take them very seriously. This counts for a lot.

Second, you talk about the specifics of their project. This ties in with your expertise. They are now in a position to discuss with you the particulars of their projects in the context of what you have to offer.

Third, you stand out from your competitors because you actually broke down what they're looking for in terms of the service you offer. This might make you look more conscientious. This can definitely make you look more professional.

Whatever the case may be, when you customize your offer instead of sending out some sort of template response, you are more likely to look distinctive in the eyes of a potential customer. Oftentimes, this is all you need to do to stand out from the crowd and get picked.

## Freelance Jobs that have Consistent Demand

The great thing about the list of freelance jobs I'm going to describe below is that they have instant demand right here, right now. You can bet that people are actively looking for these services. You don't have to wait long for people to want to hire you.

Now, I'm not saying that you are going to get hired immediately. You still have to come up with a killer profile, post up some great samples and connect with the prospective customer. In other words, you still have to sell yourself.

But with everything else being equal, these are the types of services that are sure to draw attention. So if you're going to be freelancing, you might want to look for these types of projects first.

## Freelance Jobs You can Try for Immediate Cash

If you're looking for freelance jobs or projects that pay off pretty much immediately, here's a short list. You would quickly notice that this list is pretty much similar to our discussion about Fiverr.

Please understand that buyers who frequent freelance platforms are pretty much the same people that go to Fiverr. The only big difference involves the scale of the work involved as well as the timeline.

Service buyers who go to freelance platforms instead of Fiverr are usually looking for higher quality work. They have larger projects in mind, or they're looking to establish a long term relationship. They want to find a service provider that they can go to repeatedly over an extended period of time.

In terms of the actual services that they are looking for, there's really not that much difference. Although freelance platforms involve projects that tend to be more defined and involve larger sizes.

With that said, here's the short list:

## Article Writing

One of the most commonly requested services found on freelance platforms involve article writing. This has many different versions. You can write articles, reviews, blog posts – they pretty much all flow to the same place. It's all about writing around keywords or concepts.

Since there is quite a bit of a diversity in terms of project specifications as far as article and blog post writings go, it will give you a tremendous competitive advantage if you produce material that is persuasive. Seriously.

If you're looking to sell your writing services like hotcakes, focus on being persuasive. Because when you think about it, the reason why people buy this service in the first place is because they're trying to sell something.

Maybe your article will have ads around it. Maybe your article would have a link to some sort of review from which people can then buy stuff, it all leads to the same place. Maybe the link goes to some sort of squeeze page for a mailing list.

But make no mistake about it, at the end of the day, somebody has to buy something for the publisher to have a few extra dollars in his or her bank account. That's the bottom line.

With that in mind, it will give you a tremendous advantage if your writing samples are persuasive. How do you persuade when writing articles? Well, you have to follow the right format.

If the client wants reviews, study how reviews are set up. You would notice that they tend to follow a pattern. Follow that pattern and your chances of persuading the reader goes up tremendously.

Also, read many different examples of the articles that you're supposed to write. You should be able to connect the dots. A certain pattern should emerge. You will be able to quickly tell which is a high-quality, persuasive article and which item simply goes through the motions. It doesn't really make much of an impression.

From my personal experience, high quality reviews or persuasive articles do four things. If you are able to hit these competently, don't be surprised if you have a lot of clients coming back to you again and again.

First, your article has to attract attention. It doesn't matter whether it's a review, a blog post or a formal article. It has to draw people's attention. This means your title has to be written with attention-grabbing in mind. You have to appeal to their emotions, you have to trigger their curiosity. Whatever it is, you need to grab their attention.

Second, an effective article filters the reader. The last thing that you want is to write an article on a very broad keyword and have that article try to appeal to all the people who would possibly be interested in that topic. That is impossible.

You're just wasting your time doing that because I can almost guarantee that whoever is unlucky enough to read your article will not be interested. It's too broad or it's too specific to somebody else. Whatever the case may be, they won't be happy. This is why you have to research keywords that drill down in terms of intent.

When you do keyword research for SEO purposes, you can actually cluster these different keywords based on what the person's looking for. For example, somebody who types in the search phrase "buy Nike athletic shoes" is obviously interested in buying a specific type of shoe produced by a specific manufacturer. Compare this with an article on athletic shoes. That's too broad. You don't have enough information to craft the article.

If somebody types in "buy Nike athletic shoes," you can then create a list article on how people should buy Nike shoes. What features should they look for? How do they know that they spotted high quality athletic shoes? What defines an athletic shoe that is worth their hard earned dollars?

Do you see where I'm coming from? You have to filter the reader so as to maximize their interest in your article. That's the only way you can sell them. If you fail in the filtration stage, your article is going to be a bust.

The third element is to draw a tight connection between the solutions that you mentioned in your content and the desires of the reader. As I have mentioned above, people entering search terms have a specific range of intent. The intent of a person typing in "history of athletic shoes" is going to be very different from somebody who typed in "buy athletic shoes by Nike."

Since you have a clear idea of what this range of intent is, it should also be readily apparent to you what they need. What is it that they desire? What kind of problem do they have that they're trying to solve? You should then lay out information that helps solve that problem.

This is how you awaken desire in them. You become more credible. They look through your materials and you back up whatever it is that you're saying, and this helps create the impression of authority.

They only need to scan through your article to get the impression that they should listen to you. You know what you're talking about. They should give you the benefit of the doubt. In other words, you build trust based on how well you read their intent. And this is revealed in the keywords that you target.

You have to study your keyword targets closely, pick out related keywords that create context, and build your article around awakening the desires that those keywords speak to. There has to be a tight fit between the solution that you're ultimately selling and the intent the user has.

This connection should then express itself in the form of desire. Because if somebody doesn't desire your solution, they're wasting their time. Since you're wasting their time, you're wasting your time because they're not going to buy. They're not going to click on an ad. They're not going to enter their email address on an email form. They're not going to do anything that would add dollars to your bank account.

Finally, highly effective articles draw readers to action. Now, don't get too excited. This doesn't mean that these people will automatically click on an ad to buy stuff. While that does happen, most of the time, they would want to hear more from you.

This is a tremendous opportunity. You can get them to click on a link to another article that would convince them of buying a product. You can get them to click on a link that goes to a squeeze page so they can enter their email address. Once they're on your list, you can have a long running conversation with them. You can get them to go back to your website and eventually convert them into a buyer.

There are just so many ways you can run with this. What's important is that you have to call them to action. You have to get them to engage in some sort of activity that increases the likelihood you will make money off that traffic.

This is the essence of highly effective article writing. It's all about persuasion. If your work samples are flat or they look like they were written by a machine or they're just all too generic, nobody would care.

Write to persuade because ultimately, the buyers of freelance services, regardless of the platform, are interested in generating a sale. This may not be immediate, they may be looking to get more mailing list members, but whatever the case may be, it eventually leads there. So set yourself apart from the competition by writing persuasive, authoritative and credible articles.

The downside to this, of course, is that this requires a lot more time and attention to detail. Since you're trading your time for money, you might have to charge rates that are higher than average. If that's the case, then you end up in a classic chicken or egg dilemma. For you to get orders, you have to get ratings and reviews. Unfortunately, for you to get ratings and reviews, you have to get orders in the first place.

As I have mentioned in our discussion on Fiverr, you can jump start this process by enlisting your friends, family members and coworkers to buy your article-writing services to get a nice initial list of reviews so prospective buyers would know that you're the real deal.

## Translation services

Just like with Fiverr, you can offer translation services. Make sure you're very competent in a language that is in high demand. Spanish and French are in great demand. Mandarin Chinese is also quite popular.

On the other hand, if your second language is fairly obscure or people rarely ask for translations in that language, you might not want to offer this service. You might not want to go into this. There might not be that much listings on freelance platforms for your second language. Still, it doesn't hurt to look, but the ROE or return on effort has to be there.

When making a bid, make sure you submit a translation sample. This way, this tells the prospective customer that you are serious about this translation job. Don't just say, "I know Mandarin. You should hire me." That doesn't move the ball at all.

Direct them to a link that's in Mandarin Chinese and send them a copy of a document written in Chinese script that you translated. If they know what they're doing, they should have a native Chinese speaker read your materials to see if it's in proper context or if it's fluent enough.

## Ebook Creation Services

Another common project posted on freelance platforms involve ebooks. Thanks to Amazon's Kindle library and places like Clickbank or JVZoo, a lot of clients ask for custom ebook writing services. They give you a topic or a proposed table of contents and you research materials for the book. You send your initial abstract or proposal to them, they approve, and then you write out the book.

You have to protect yourself when offering this type of service. You don't want to go through the time, effort and hassle of coming up with a 40,000-word book, which took you weeks to write, only to have the customer ask for an impossible round of revisions. You're going to find yourself in an impossible situation where you've wasted all this time only not to get paid.

Even if you were to get paid, if you get trapped in an endless cycle of revisions, you've effectively worked way below minimum wage because instead of freeing up that time to take on other clients, you just spent all your available effort writing a book for just one customer.

It's also a good idea to have ebook samples ready for prospective customers. You have to have a link to your past work. You have to show them what you've done before.

Also, when looking for ebook writing opportunities on freelance platforms, zero in on requests that fall within your range of expertise. For example, if you know nothing about cooking, much less Tibetan cuisine, you have no business putting in a bid for a Tibetan cookbook. I hope you get my point.

Write about what you know, or write about what you are curious about. This way, when you're going through the research and writing process, it doesn't feel like you're pulling teeth. It actually feels like an exciting adventure, and you're more likely to come up with a superior product.

Now, the secret to successful ebook writing boils down to getting repeat orders. If you get an order and you hit the ball out of the park, maybe you over delivered in terms of word count or quality, chances are quite good your customer will not only come back, but spread the word about your service. That's exactly the kind of situation you want.

If ebook writing seems like a hassle to you, there is a shortcut you can take. You can sign up for a PLR membership at one of the larger PLR collections available online. This way, when you check out their PLR books that fit the topic of your assignment, you can get the initial research out of the way.

Now, chances are quite good that these PLR books would have covered 70-80% of what you need to talk about in your custom ebook writing project. This makes research so much easier because now you only have to cover 20% in new research. You end up saving a lot of time and effort. Using PLR to get initial ideas can even get you a competitive advantage because you can promise to deliver custom written ebooks in a shorter time.

## Warning

When using PLR, make sure you do not copy and paste. This is very tempting because a lot of freelance book writers are under the impression that since these books are not going to be published online, the owner has no way of knowing when you copied and pasted portions from PLR. Resist that temptation.

Based on my experience, Amazon has a technology that enables it to check the text of Kindle formatted books against online sources. It may not be perfect yet, but you don't want to run that risk. You don't want to ruin your reputation as a freelance writer by plagiarizing somebody else's work. PLR is supposed to just give you ideas and initial facts. The rest is up to you.

## Editing Projects

A lot of people confuse editing with proofreading. They are two totally different animals. When somebody says that they want a proofreading, this is actually a pretty easy project.

What you need to do is copy and paste the text of the article, book or blog post into software like Whitesmoke or Grammarly to get a good idea of the grammar quality of the content. These software tools will tell you if there's something off.

Now, you cannot automatically trust the software. Sometimes they return false positives. You still have to read the text and manually proof it, but software definitely makes your job easier by saving you time.

If a client is asking for editing services, you must charge more money. Editing is very different from proofreading because when you edit, you're looking for flow. You're reading the item as a whole. This is especially complicated for a book. You're reading everything in context. You're also looking for holes in the text.

Maybe the author made a claim, but failed to back it up. Maybe they gave some sort of evidence that doesn't seem to fit. Whatever the case may be, there are certain things missing from the book. Your job as an editor is to highlight these holes and bring it to the attention of the client.

Depending on the kind of editing job you took on, it may be your responsibility to plug in those holes. Of course, the more intensive the editing job, the more you can charge.

## Producing Presentations

There are lots of people who need to make PowerPoint presentations for their work. Unfortunately, many people do not have the skills, the time or the patience to create powerful slideshows. This is where you come in.

You can come up with slides using PowerPoint. You can even use the Open Office Suite so you don't have to spend money on Microsoft Office. You can just export it in PPT format so your customer can load it on to PowerPoint.

Presentations can help you make good money because they involve writing, research analysis, as well as picture selection and slideshow creation. You can even include video elements as well.

Make sure that you size up different presentation projects correctly, though. Don't assume that you will be able to find public domain or "fair use" pictures very quickly. This is the part of the presentation creation process that tends to slow down freelancers quite a bit. They assume that the pictures are all over the place and they find out in the worst way possible that this is not the case. Don't do that.

When going through the different project listings, do a quick search on Google Image search and select the public domain or the usage rights option to look for public domain or legally usable images. Also, you need to send a private message to the client asking them if they're willing to pay for royalty-free stock images. This can definitely speed up the slide show presentation creation process.

## Offer Custom Photography

Another common service requested at freelance platforms involve custom photography. Customers from all over the world are looking for all sorts of custom photos for a wide range of books, marketing campaigns, articles, blog posts, and other types of content.

Royalty-free stock photo sites simply do not have the photos that they're looking for. Do yourself a big favor and look for stock photography freelance projects. You'd be surprised as to how easy this is.

Now, here's one piece of advice. If you're going to be taking pictures of people, make sure you get them to sign a release. If they don't sign a general release, you might be on the hook for a lot of money. They can sue you for stealing their image or selling the rights to their image. Make sure you get them to sign a release.

# Money Making Method #3: Freelance Writing

The demand for custom text content is so pervasive and so common that I had to create a special section just for freelance writing.

There are many different places online where you can get freelance writing jobs. I've already covered Fiverr, where you create an offer, and I've also covered freelance writing platforms. On those platforms, you look for projects posted by potential clients asking for freelance writing services.

Those are just two places. You can also look at classified ad websites like Craigslist. You can also look at forums like Warrior Forum, Digital Point, and Black Hat World. Online publishers of all stripes and sizes are constantly looking for freelance writers.

Now, a lot of them don't pay all that well, so make sure you know exactly what you're getting into. Writing reviews, for example, is not very easy. This is why it's really important to make sure you have the format down before you offer freelance writing services. The format for an effective article is different from a format for an effective blog post.

It's also important for you to specialize. The more specialized your content, the higher the chance you will get higher paying customers.

Two of the most lucrative sub niches in the freelance writing space are email writing and sales page writing. There's a huge amount of demand for these specialized writing services because very few people know how to create compelling emails and sales pages. That's just the reality. Chances are, you've seen many different sales pages as you have browsed the internet. Chances are, you did not buy from the vast majority of them.

You have to be very competent in specialized forms of writing for you to have a fighting chance at getting a lucrative writing side hustle going. You can make quite a bit of money, but the key here is to focus on making as much money for as little effort as possible. This is why specialization is key.

Steer clear of low paying writing jobs. For example, SEO writing tends to pay much lower than sales page or email writing. Generic blog post writing also isn't that rewarding.

Don't get me wrong, this side hustle can still be worth it if you live in a developing country with a low cost of living and the dollar exchange rate is very high. In that situation, you may be able to live comfortably off article and blog post writing.

However, if you live in the United States, Canada, Western Europe, New Zealand or Australia, you might want to step up. You might want to study websites like backlinko.com and moz.com and master the art of high quality article and blog post writing. That's the only way you can have a fighting chance to get paid high enough rates that make a freelance writing side hustle worth it.

As I mentioned above, you can also look into specializing on email or sales page writing. To get the proper training, you might want to check out sites like copyblogger.com and do research on persuasive writing. Nail the format and study how to write for SEO.

Also, if you're going to specialize in writing reviews, read tons of product reviews. Try to zero in on the more effective ones, and reverse engineer them. This doesn't mean that you're just going to rewrite them. Instead, pay attention to why they are so persuasive.

## Amazon MTurk

Another side hustle that pays off almost immediately is Amazon MTurk. MTurk enables you to earn really quick cash. The problem is, it pays very little. In fact, its human intelligence tasks or HITs can pay as little as 3 cents per task.

These are very small tasks that people can easily do. Maybe you're supposed to find a number on a page, or maybe you're supposed to count something. They don't take all that much time. They're very easy, but they do require some sort of analysis. The problem is, they pay so little.

One way you can actually make money off MTurk is to do as many tasks as you can. Now, this may still not be worth it because of exchange rates.

If you live in the United States, by and large, MTurk just pays too little. Stay away from HITs. It's just not worth it. But if you live in a developing country, the ROE or return on effort might be there. It all depends on how many small tasks you take on.

## Microworkers

Another website that you can check out is microworkers.com. They pay a little bit more than MTurk. It's not unusual to get paid 10, 15, or even 25 cents per action. Tasks include account creation, clicking on links, posting links on your blog, and other small tasks.

Now, please note that my analysis on MTurk applies to Microworkers and similar platforms. Pay attention to your return on effort. Make sure that you spend as little time doing the work while trying to get paid as much as possible.

There are pay per click services available in the United States. Make sure that you have a USIP address, however. They are very particular about that. Your IP address must be geographically located in the United States. They may also try to qualify in a number of ways. But they can pay quite well.

Some places pay as much as a dollar per click, but the drawback is that they don't give you that many tasks. Sure, you get paid $1 per click, but the problem is, you only have one click per day, so in this case, you might want to look for as many of these different sites as possible so you can at least make $10, $15 or $20 per day. It's not much money, but it's a side hustle that doesn't take up much of your time.

# SECTION 2

# Side Hustles That Can Pay Off Within a Week Or So

In the previous category of side hustles, I focused on hustles that pay off almost immediately. For example, you just need to go to a freelance platform, look at the projects on offer, and make a bid. You then send work samples, and if the client picks you, you have yourself a project. Complete that project and you get paid.

In the case of Fiverr, put together a nice and very attractive profile. If you pick the right gig to offer, chances are, you can start generating sales immediately.

In this set of side hustles, however, expect to wait for some time. You either have to create sites that you're going to sell or you are going to drive traffic to a page, and when that traffic converts, you make money.

# Side Hustle Idea #1: Become a link broker

This technique is a simple buy low, sell high money making side hustle. Please understand that people are always looking for links for SEO purposes. While Google has evolved quite a bit, it's still very dependent on backlinks in ranking websites.

People know this. So when they buy domain names that have a lot of high quality backlinks, and they reinstall WordPress to create a blog on that domain name, they can "resurrect" the backlink power or SEO "juice" of that domain name.

People buy links embedded in the posts of those blogs for SEO purposes. You can go to websites such as Black Hat World and look for such service providers.

Next, you can post ads on Craigslist and other online classified ads websites advertising your link placement service. You tell them the SEO features of the links in the network that you're reselling. Usually, these include the following:

Number of referring backlinks – This metric comes from AHREFS.com

Domain authority (DA) – This metric comes from Moz.com

Page authority (PA) – This metric comes from Moz.com

Trust flow (TF) – This metric comes from Majestic.com

Citation Flow (CF) – This metric comes from Majestic.com

Without getting too technical, generally speaking, the higher these numbers, the more valuable the link source is. So your job is to find link sellers that offer links from networks that have a very high SEO profile. You then sell these links through classified ads. You should put up a sales page describing the SEO qualities of the network you're selling and how much each link costs.

This is active income, but the good news is, you don't really spend that much time. You're just waiting for the orders to come in and you send out an email to the link sellers.

I know people who make thousands of dollars every single month simply flipping link sales. Ideally, you should advertise to attract the attention of newbies who don't really know SEO all that well. At the very least, they don't know it enough to go to the places where you're buying these links from. You're just being a middleman.

## Side Hustle Tip #1: Sell pre-made blogs

A lot of people want to earn a passive income publishing online. When you have a blog and post ads on it, you don't have to post every day. You can post to the blog and drive traffic to it. While you're working your 9 to 5 job or doing something else, people visit the blog. And if they like an ad, they click on it.

Depending on the ads that you run, you can actually make money when people click or leave their email address or click through the product being sold and buy the product. You usually get an affiliate commission when you run affiliate ads. That's how powerful and passive blogging for money can be.

Now, not everybody knows how to do this. This is where you come in. You just set up the blog and fill it with content. You then place it for sale on certain places on the internet and people buy it from you.

You can easily make several times the value of the time you spent building the blog. People don't want to start from scratch, so they'd rather buy something that already exists.

Here's how selling pre-made blogs work:

## Find a Hot Niche

The first thing that you need to do if you are going to be making money selling pre-made blogs is to create blogs that you know people would buy.

How would you know? Well, there are two ways to do this. You can do extensive research based on your personal interests and analyze traffic data. This is the harder way to do it because it takes a lot more time.

The good news here is that you can isolate niches that may make quite a bit of money. If you find a buyer who can recognize the value of that niche, they might buy your pre-made blog from you.

The downside to this is that the return on effort might not be there. You spend time looking for the right niche, analyzing it, creating content, putting the blog together, and there is a chance that people might not want to buy it because they are not familiar with it.

I know that sounds like a dumb reason, but that's what happens quite a bit in places where sites are bought and sold. Thankfully, there is an easier way.

## Reverse Engineer Niches

The shortcut is to reverse engineer niches for blogs that are already selling. You only need to go to flippa.com. Look for starter blogs that are being sold. Pay attention to when the item was listed and when it sells.

If you notice that certain websites sell out really quickly, you should pay attention. Try to see if they fit a particular niche.

If you notice that certain blog niches tend to sell out really fast, that's the niche you need to be in. Just copy the niche.

Pay attention to the characteristics of the website. If the domain name of the site is listed, go to the site. Pay attention to how many posts it has. look at the content it contains, whether it has a lot of pictures or not, and look at the categories it has. Take a lot of notes.

Once you have a clear understanding of what sells in terms of niche, number of posts or pages, and types of content on the blog like pictures, videos or any other type of content format, the next step is to create your own version.

## Reverse Engineer Your Target Niches to Find Keywords to Focus On

Now that you have done extensive research on Flippa and you know which niches sell, the next step is to go to Google's keyword planner tool and look for keywords related to those niches. You should be able to get a ton of keywords. The key here is to come up with a cluster of keywords that would provide a context for a workable blog.

This blog has to have a context. For example, if you notice that a lot of forex starter blogs sell out really quickly on Flippa, you know that you should be in the forex space. That much is obvious. But you also need to look at how they present forex.

Are these websites helping people to learn the ropes of forex? Are they reviewing forex platforms? What exactly do they do? How do they position the niche?

When you do your keyword research, you should be able to come up with keywords that will help you specialize within that niche. This way, when you sell the website, it is based around keywords that give it a context. This not only helps you get more traffic from search engines, but it also makes it easier for people who are looking to buy your blog to size up your blog.

They can see that you've done your research, they can see that you are targeting the different content areas within your niche, so it's more likely that they would think that you know what you're talking about, or at least that the blog looks legit.

It also helps to do keyword research because you may want to post up AdSense ads. These are triggered by the keywords of your articles and, depending on the keywords, these might pay quite a bit of money per click. There is actually a lot of demand for AdSense-powered blogs on Flippa.

## How to Select Keywords

Now that you have a rough idea of the kind of keywords that you're working with, you're going to have to sort through your keywords. Follow the steps below:

## Sort by Intent

The first thing that you need to do is to sort all the keywords you have based on the intent or context of those words. Remember, you're building a niche blog. The keywords have to be about a specific subtopic. Get rid of everything else.

## Filter by Search Volume

The next thing that you're going to do is you're going to pick out keywords based on how often they get searched within a month.

Here's the trick: don't pick the most popular ones. I can almost guarantee there's going to be a tremendous amount of competition for those keywords. It's going to be very hard for you to rank your website. Look for something in the middle.

You don't want to target low traffic keywords either because nobody's searching for them. You're not going to get much search engine traffic. Shoot for something in the middle.

## Filter Your Remaining Keywords by Commercial Value

Google's keyword planner tool shows you the cost per click of each keyword. Filter out overly cheap keywords. What's left should be the keywords that you're going to base your website on.

## Use Your Remaining Keywords to Structure Your Site

You should have a fairly short list of remaining keywords. Now, conceptually analyze those keywords to create a structure for your site. This is going to be the navigation system for your site.

Some keywords would make for great categories, other keywords would make for keyword targets for articles that fall within categories. Structure your website this way.

## How Do You Create Quality Content?

Now, here's the most important step. Screw this up, and your blog flipping career will die in a fire. Seriously. Because you may be able to sell your first blog, but if people don't make money on it, chances are, you're not going to sell another blog. You'll develop a bad reputation for creating duds.

You need people to see the value of your product. It must be readily apparent. This means that you have to create quality content.

You can't just get a list of keywords, hire somebody from the other side of the planet who could barely write to piece together an article around those keywords, and then this content doesn't make any sense. That will not help your pre-made blog sell.

Instead, take your article keywords and follow the steps below. I've used this method to find tried and proven content that blows away my competition each and every time. My secret? Reverse engineering!

## Step #1: Find your competitors
The first thing that you need to do is to enter your target keywords into Google to find your competitors. Get a list of their websites.

## Step #2: Find their most popular content
Now that you have identified your keyword competitors, find their most popular content. How do you know? Well, you can see from social signals.

If you notice that a lot of their content gets shared a lot or has retweets or ranks on Google Plus, then you know that that content is popular on social media. Get a list of all the content that is popular which are produced by your competitors. This should be a long list of content.

The next step is to run these specific URLs through backlink checker tools like ahrefs.com or majestic.com. These tools will show you how many other websites link to those articles.

At this point, you have an idea of how popular these URLs are on social media, and now you're going to filter them based on how popular they are with other blogs. The remaining articles are the ones that you're going to reverse engineer.

## Step #3: Copy their topics to create your own version

This is extremely important. You're going to copy what they're talking about, but you're not just going to reword the article. I hope that's clear. You're going to make a better version.

How? Make sure that the titles grab attention while mentioning your keyword. Make sure they're dramatic or they leave space for the imagination. Whatever the case may be, get people to click on the title.

Also, invest in better pictures. When people share this content on social media, these pictures are automatically published. These pictures must grab attention. What works for me are header pictures that have text in them that ask questions or get people emotionally triggered.

You have to understand that people share content on social media like Facebook all day, every day. Your stuff has to stand out. If it means that you have to use graphical headers with text titles on them, do it.

## Write Content for SEO

Not only should your content attract attention, but it also has to attract Google's attention. So you have to write for SEO.

I use Yoast SEO WordPress plug-in. This WordPress plug-in will tell me my keyword saturation as well as the placement of my keywords. It optimizes my content for SEO. When you use that plug-in, you're pretty much 80% of the way there in terms of search engine optimization.

## Step #4: Format your text to be read

I don't know about you, but I hate reading massive blocks of text. Who has the time? Plus, it also looks scary. It's a massive commitment when you're supposed to read 200 words in one scary looking blog.

You should format your text so it's easy to read. Meaning, you write in short, choppy sentences. Each paragraph should be no longer than three sentences. Feel free to use one sentence paragraphs.

Also, in between your text blocks, include pictures, diagrams or even videos. Within the sentences, make sure you use different fonts like bold font and then italics. Do whatever you can to make the text interesting.

Please understand that people are in a hurry. Often times, they are going to be reading your content using a mobile device like a tablet or a phone. It's not like they have all the patience and time in the world, so make it worth their while.

A good model for this is backlinko.com. Look at how Brian formats his content. You should do something similar. Now, please understand that it's okay to publish really long posts.

## Step #5: Use long posts

According to statistical analysis of millions of blog posts, those posts that tend to be longer and presented in one page tend to rank higher. This is not speculation. This is based on hard data analysis.

So resist the temptation of taking a 2,000-word post and then splitting it up into different pages. That's very annoying – where people have to click the next page link to see what's next. People won't even read your stuff.

When they see a "next" link, they would go to your competitor's website and read their stuff because they can't be bothered to read yours. So put everything in one page, but format it so it's a joy to read.

## Basic Blogging Housekeeping

A lot of side hustle books go through the long technical details of setting up a blog, buying a domain name and other steps. I'm not going to rip you off that way. Because if you're reading this, you should already know that if you're going to be selling a pre-made blog, you're going to have to get hosting and you're going to have to buy a domain name. You also have to install WordPress.

The good news is that you can easily buy hosting for a few dollars every month. It's very cheap. Also, WordPress is free. In fact, a lot of hosting accounts allow you to install WordPress just by clicking a button. You click a button, you type in the name of your website along with other details, and you're good to go.

When you buy a domain name, you must point it to the DNS server of your host. That's all you need to do. If you need further details on this, just do a search on it. It's pretty straightforward.

There are tons of articles on this. I'm not going to rip you off by wasting precious space in this book giving you stuff that you can easily find. But you need to do this. This is basic housekeeping stuff, so you can then sell your blog to your buyer.

## Selling Your Blog on Flippa

There are other places you can use to sell online properties. You can use latona.com, empireflippers.com, and there are other boutique website sales platforms.

What I like about Flippa is that it's the biggest player in the website resale space. It's the 800-pound gorilla. Nobody even comes close. So if you want to reach the largest possible group of buyers, start with Flippa.

Maybe when you've gotten really good at this and you are creating premium websites, you can then try those other options. They do pay a lot more, but your website really has to produce results. But if you're just selling websites with no traffic, you really can't go wrong with Flippa.

## Create a Flippa Listing

If you're just starting out, you need to create a profile that sets people at ease. As you can probably already tell, there are lots of rip offs on the internet. Some shady characters have used Flippa in the past to rip off buyers. Understand that this is the case, so people can be quite suspicious. Your job is to set them at ease.

How do you do that? Well, your profile should show your actual face. It should show the real name of your company or reveal details that basically tell the reader that you are a real person and that they can trust you. You're not playing any games, you're not using aliases, and you're not pulling any sort of shenanigans to separate them from their money.

Your listing must set people at ease. How do you do this? Well, you should list out, in clear terms, what your niche is, how many pages of content there is, and how many words. You can show screenshots and you should also show the URL. This way, when people go to your website, they can see that the website is quality.

Now, understand that starter websites don't have to look like works of art, but they cannot look like junk either. This is why you should invest in a good theme for your WordPress blog for it to sell well.

The good news is that this doesn't have to cost you an arm and a leg. You can get a custom theme done at Fiverr for a fairly low amount of money. You can then recycle that theme after making a few changes to the colors and layout for your future projects. This way, you pay only once, but you make use of the theme many times over.

## Price Your Product Right

The secret here is to not get greedy. Since you've reverse engineered your niche, you should have a clear idea of how much, on average, your type of website sells for. Stay within that average. Don't get too greedy.

Right now, you really haven't proven yourself. You don't really have a reputation for producing a long line of high quality sites that actually pull traffic. At this point, your main focus should be just to sell the site. Your main focus should be just to get your first sale.

So it's perfectly okay to price your first starter blog on the lower end of the scale. Since you've already done research as to the wide range of prices, then shoot for the lower end.

## Use Escrow

If you priced your pre-made site correctly, you should be able to sell the website fairly quickly. At this stage, you have to protect yourself. You should use an escrow service like escrow.com.

The buyer would put the money in the escrow. You would then send the log in information as well as data to your buyer. Your buyer then should be able to take your WordPress files as well as domain name and install it on his or her server.

For a cleaner transfer, you might want to consider transferring the complete website from your host to your buyer's server. Depending on who you host with, this is actually pretty easy. You just need to make a request. Some hosting companies would even do this for free.

Whatever the case may be, make sure that the money is in the escrow, and once you've transferred everything, give the buyer a time limit when they can inspect the website. Once that time limit is up, you get the money from escrow. Make sure to document everything so you don't get ripped off.

## Pro Tip Writing Content

The Achilles heel or the weak spot of this side hustle is writing the content. Unless you are a prolific writer who can pretty much write at a drop of a hat and produce thousands of words every day, writing can be a hassle. Not everybody's a natural writer.

How do you make money selling pre-made blogs if you can't generate content? It's actually quite simple. You just outsource this task.

You can go to places like Freelancer.com or Upwork to find a freelancer to produce the content for you, or you can find a writer on Fiverr. It's very important that you take a look at their work quality, so you can have a good idea of what to expect. You can also try low cost native English speaking service providers like ozki.org.

Regardless of which way you go, make sure that the content fits the standards of the websites you're reverse engineering. Outsourcing definitely saves you a lot of time.

## Side Hustle Tip #2: CPA

CPA stands for cost per acquisition or cost per action. These ads appear on your blog, and when people click it, you don't get paid. People have to fill out a form for you to get paid. They have to complete an action.

Usually, these ads offer some sort of free gift, and when people click on the ad to get the free gift, they have to enter their email address or put in their zip code.

Believe or not, when people complete an offer form, CPA ads can pay quite a bit of money. It's not uncommon for people to make thousands of dollars every day off of CPA. That's how lucrative CPA ads are.

The downside to CPA is traffic. I'm not talking about you being able to drive traffic to your blog. That's a given. You have to do that. Instead, your traffic has to be the right kind of traffic.

CPA ads only work really well if you get a lot of traffic from the United States, the United Kingdom, or other top tier countries.

On the other hand, if most of your traffic comes from China, India, the Philippines and other places, CPA ads either pay very little or are not available at all. When people click on the ad, the form doesn't even show up because their IP address is not a top tier country.

Keep this in mind when considering this side hustle. If you're sure that you can get top tier or Tier 1 traffic, then you should definitely look into doing CPA.

## Step #1: Join a CPA network

There are quite a number of CPA networks you can join. The two biggest are maxbounty.com and peerfly.com. Once you have joined the network, you will get access to codes. These are URLs that have your affiliate code.

What can you do with these codes? The key is to publish the code on the internet so that when people click it, they end up on the CPA form. If they fill out the form, you make money. If they don't, you don't make money. Pretty simple.

Thankfully, there are many ways you can promote your CPA link.

## CPA Side Hustle Method #1: Blog

The simplest way you can make money off CPA is to just follow the steps I gave you for creating a blog that you will flip. Look at the earlier side hustle method. Just go through those steps. Do keyword selection, install the blog, post content—just go through the whole process. The only thing that's different is you're going to use CPA ads all over your blog.

The great thing about CPA ads compared to AdSense is that they're more liberal as to where you can put them. You can pretty much fill up your whole blog with ads if you want, but I don't recommend that. You will suffer a search engine penalty from Google's update called Panda if you do that. But you definitely are given a freer hand with ad placements if you use CPA ads instead of AdSense.

The next thing that you need to do when using blogs for CPA is to drive traffic. In driving traffic, your only limit, really is your imagination. Here's a short list of the things you can do to drive traffic to your blog:

## SEO

You can build links to your website using guest posts and outreach to get your site's name and other links to appear on other websites. If you keep this up long enough, you may rank higher for your target keywords.

## Comments

Believe it or not, blog comments still work. You can't be lazy, though. The comment has to actually add value to the blog post you're commenting on. You actually have to discuss something. But if people see that the link to your article adds value or contains information that they're looking for, they might click through and might click on a CPA ad.

## Forums

Forums like Reddit, as well as forum-like platforms like Facebook groups, can be great sources of traffic as well. Again, it really all boils down to the comments that you post. You must post content. You can't just post a link and call it a day. That's not going to work. You have to actually contribute.

## Facebook Ads

Facebook ads are paid ads. You're going to have to pay for this traffic. The good news is, if you run many experiments on Facebook swapping out different pictures and different texts, you may be able to lower your cost per click. The secret here is to find groups that cater to your blog's niche.

Once you have found those groups and you joined them, look at the profiles of the people that joined those groups. In particular, look at the things that they like. Make a list of the pages that they like. Pay attention to their interests.

Using this information, when you're putting out your ad, copy the same interests. Sometimes, the interests are given as an option by the Facebook ads, sometimes they're not. So just put in as many different interests that you've researched from these people.

This way, your ads will be better targeted, and this can lead to you paying less per click, but getting quality clicks. This can increase the chances that people going to your blog are more likely to click on your CPA ads.

## CPA Side Hustle Method #2: Post videos on YouTube

Now that you have written articles for your blog post, see if you can create slide shows based on them.

If you know somebody who has a pleasant voice, maybe you can create a short script for them and they can do a voice explainer video. Maybe it can be three to five minutes. However you do it, come up with videos and then post this stuff on YouTube. In certain parts of the video, direct the viewer to click on the link in the description.

The great thing about using YouTube to promote your CPA-powered blog is that it's usually easier to rank on YouTube than on Google's regular search engine. Of course, this depends on how competitive your niche is.

If you are targeting a blog niche that everybody and his dog is trying to dominate, then you're probably not going to have much luck with YouTube. But if you are in a fairly decent competitive niche, you may be able to rank some of your videos highly.

You shouldn't just upload your video and forget about it. You should also promote your video on social media platforms.

If your videos are high quality and they talk about information that people are really interested in, go to Facebook groups, Google Plus communities and Twitter and spread your YouTube video link. You'd be surprised as to how popular your video can be once you get it in front of the right eyeballs. If people find value in your video, don't be surprised if they share it.

# SECTION 3

# Side Hustles That Require Months To Pay Off

In this section, I'm going to cover making money with side hustles that will take quite some time. We're talking about at least three months or more.

The great thing about these two side hustles is that they're passive. You don't have to babysit them. You don't have to do work just to get paid. You don't have to trade in your time for money.

Unlike freelancing in which you don't get paid if you don't work, blogging or online publishing pretty much operates in the background. You just create a blog, and when people come into your site and click around, you can make money.

You don't have to be there to earn that money. If you build enough of these blogs, you might have a decent flow of cash that you didn't actively work for. You worked once, but that previous work generates cash pretty much throughout the year.

Now, the cash flow may not be consistent, this is why you need to scale it up by creating many different blogs. You might think that each of these creates a small amount of cash each, but let me tell you, even small trickles of cash, when you add them together, can produce a nice river of income.

# Blogging

For these steps, disregard the build and sell steps that I've taught you before. You're going to do things a bit differently.

## How does It Work?

To make money with blogging, you just post up content. This content is shown with ads around it. When users click on an ad, you make money per click or you make money per sale.

Sometimes, the ads would show an email collection box. When people join your mailing list, you make money through a CPA system.

Also, you can show an email collection box so when people join your mailing list, you can send them updates to bring them back to your site. When they go back to your website, they can click on ads that can make you money.

Alternatively, you can send offers directly to your mailing list, and if they click on an offer and they buy something, you make money directly. Make no mistake about it, you can make quite a bit of money off your email list.

## This is All Passive Income

The great thing about blogging is that it is passive income. You work only once, but it generates money on the side. You only write the blog post once, but it has the potential of making you money as long as your website is up. Not a bad proposition as long as you know how to drive traffic.

## Find the Right Niche

The secret to succeeding with blogging is to target the right niche. Since you're not going to be flipping this blog and you're going to hang on to it for the long haul, you must be interested in it. If you're not interested in your blog, the chances of you making money off of it is going to be very low.

The following steps make sure that you are going to be able to maintain this blog and eventually make money off it.

## Step #1: List your personal interests

Off the top of your head, list down all the topics that you're interested in. Don't worry about whether your answers are right or wrong. Just make sure that you list down all the things that you are interested in.

Here's a rule of thumb that I use: I would list down all the topics that I would continue to talk and write about even if I'm not getting paid. So get a long list going.

## Step #2: Research your topic's commercial value using Google's keyword planner tool

Go to Google AdWords and use the keyword planner tool to enter all the topics that you are personally interested in. You will be able to see the cost per click or click value of keywords related to those topics. This should give you a fairly rough idea of how much each topic is worth.

Cross off your list topics that have very low commercial value. The remaining niches should have a high enough commercial value.

## Step #3: Filter your list by monthly search volume

When you're using the Google keyword planner tool, it will also tell you how many people searched for that term in the space of a month on average. Eliminate keywords that have very high search volumes. Those are usually very competitive and are not worth your time.

By the same token, you should also get rid of keywords that have very little search volume. They're not worth your time. Focus on keywords that are in the middle of the road. They get decent search volumes.

A good rule of thumb is at least 1,500 to 5,000 searches per month, depending on your niche.

## Step #4: Filter your niche list by competition level

Now that you have a good idea of the keywords that are related to the niches you have remaining on your list, enter these keywords on Google. Pay attention to how many websites target those keywords. Cross off keywords that are too competitive. These are keywords that too many websites are trying to target.

## Step #5: Cross off niches that are invisible on social media

At this point, you should have a fairly short list. You're going to apply one more filter. Using related keywords to those niches, go on social media platforms like Facebook, Twitter, Pinterest, Instagram, Google Plus and whatnot, and search for accounts, groups or communities that target those keywords. If you cannot find them at all on social media, cross them off your list.

At the end of this process, you should be left with niches that you are personally interested in, has high enough commercial value, high enough search volume, manageable levels of competition, and readily available social media discussion platforms. These niches are already being discussed on social media. There are actual groups dedicated to them.

## Build Your Blog

The next step is to build your blog. Again, I'm not going to dwell into the technical details here because you can pretty much find this easily online.

First, you need to buy a domain name. I would suggest you buy a domain name that is easy to remember and fairly short. This is very important because at some point in time, you're going to try to brand your blog. It's easier to do this when you are dealing with a shorter name.

Get hosting. Ideally, you should get hosting from a service provider that can accommodate many blogs. So if you're successful with your first few blogs, you may be able to scale this up to hundreds of blogs.

I know people who actually have massive networks. We're talking hundreds, if not thousands of blogs. Now each of those blogs may only produce cents or, if they're lucky, a few bucks every day, but since they have thousands of these websites, you can see that they have very fat paydays.

Once your hosting is set up, connect your hosting service to your domain by changing your domain name's DNS server to match your hosting company's DNS server. Add your domain name to your hosting account and you should be able to install WordPress. Install WordPress with a few mouse clicks and keystrokes.

## Invest in a Solid Theme

I can't emphasize this enough. You must invest in a solid WordPress theme.

Your WordPress theme must ensure that your content is a joy to read. You don't want a theme that looks like it came out of the year 2000. You don't want a theme that looks so cheap that people don't trust your content.

Remember, the goal here is to get people to visit your website, read your content, and possibly click on ads. If you have a very distracting theme, that's going to get in the way.

It's a good idea to invest in less than $100 on a custom theme design. Just make sure you instruct the theme designer to let you know how to customize the design's look every time you reinstall the theme on your growing blog network.

This way, you're not using very basic themes for your blog network. Instead, you have this really professional looking theme, but they're different enough from each other because you customized different attributes like color, font and whatnot.

## Post Only Winning Content

Now that you have your blog set up, your next job is to make sure that you post only content that your target audience would want to read. Thankfully, this is easier than you think.

You can choose to do things the hard way and come up with guesses as to what would be hot content. Good luck with that. That approach rarely works.

The best way to do this is to find your competitors online and reverse engineer them. Here's how you do it.

## Step #1: Load all your target keywords into Google and find all the websites that target those keywords

Come up with a massive list. I'm talking about hundreds of websites.

## Steps #2: Load each site and find their winning content

Load all the websites and look through their content. See which ones have a lot of social media signals. Look at their posts. Find posts that get a lot of tweets, retweets, Facebook likes, and other indication of social media popularity.

For our present purposes, this should be good enough, but if you really want to be sure, you might want to take an extra step and cross reference these popular posts with backlink checking tools like ahrefs.com to see how many other third party sites are linking to these pieces of content. Obviously, the more blogs link to a content, the higher its appeal.

## Step #3: Reverse engineer the topics of your remaining list

Now that you have a list of content winners, analyze their topics and come up with your own version.

## Step #4: Improve the content

How do you improve your competitor's winning content? Well, it's actually pretty easy. You can offer up to date information, you can offer more information in terms of longer posts, you can format this information better so it's easier to read, and you can include multimedia elements like graphics, diagrams, and videos. Whatever you do, make sure that the content you come up with is obviously superior to the stuff that you're reverse engineering.

It also helps, from an SEO standpoint, to offer really long content. According to hard core statistical analysis, blog posts that are 1,500 to 2,000 words tend to get more love from Google. So invest in longer content.

Also, make sure that you format that content as long form content. Meaning, you don't break it up into small pages that people have to click the "next page" link to see the next page. That's very annoying. Don't do that.

Instead, offer all the content in one page. This increases your chances of pulling more traffic from search engines.

## Promote Your Blog Posts

Creating your content is just the beginning. You're wasting your time if you're just going to write a blog post and forget about it. You have to also have a system for promoting your content. Here's how I do it:

## Step #1: Create social media accounts

The first thing I do is I create an account on all the major social media platforms. The covers for these must look professional. They must look legit. They can't look temporary.

## Step #2: Open an auto-poster account

There are services like hootsuite.com and socialoomph.com. These services take your content and publishes it on your social media accounts on a scheduled basis.

Now, here's the trick. You're going to look for the best content created by your competitors. You should already have this since you reverse engineered your competitors. You should already have a massive list of their top notch content. Feed this into your auto-posters and then, every once in a while, set it up so that it posts your own original content.

Why do this? Why promote your competitors? Well, actually, you're creating credibility among the people who are interested in your niche on all those social media platforms. When they see that you're only posting the very best stuff in your niche, they are more likely to follow your social media account. Set up your social poster so operate over several months.

## Step #3: Create derivative content

Create derivative content based on your own materials. Maybe you can create infographics out of them. You can get custom graphic diagrams done. You might even get slideshows done. Whatever the case may be, post them on your website and then rotate the links to that content on your auto-posters on social media.

At this point, your social media accounts are then going to be showing your original posts as well as derivative content. These are pictures, videos, links to infographics and other stuff.

## Step #4: Reach out to other bloggers

Reach out on social media to other bloggers in your niche. Engage with them, comment on their content. Try to be friends with them. Eventually, ask for guest posts. Ask them if you can write a blog post that they can post on their website.

What do you get out of it? You get a link back to your blog. If you keep this up enough times, your search engine rankings can go up.

Also, ask them if you can interview them. This is a very powerful way of getting backlinks because people are very egotistic. If you interview somebody, there's a good chance they might link to the interview. You're not necessarily linking to them, but they can link to you because they want their followers to know that they are being interviewed.

You can also interact with other bloggers regarding blog round ups. These are questions that some bloggers ask and people chip in answers and somebody publishes it on their blog. It's a great way to get links.

Do whatever you can to promote your brand. It doesn't have to be much, but as long as you're consistent, eventually, the overall ability of your blog to attract traffic from the internet, whether through social media, people sharing your link, or through search engines, scales up over time.

# Conclusion

Whether you need cash immediately or would like to build a long term asset, I've given you the inside scoop on side hustles you can work on right here, right now. Best of all, most if not all of these side hustle ideas won't burn a hole through your pocket to build. Get started today and start scaling up your income! Turn your spare time into spare cash!

# About The Author

Mike Jones is a digital marketing expert and entrepreneur with more than 15 years of communications and marketing experience. Jones is the founder of a number of successful e-commerce websites and My Managed Content, a marketing company that works to boost B2B and B2C brands, so that they have a solid online presence that reaches their intended audiences.

Learn more about what Mike and his team can do for your business or brand at MyManagedContent.com.

www.ingramcontent.com/pod-product-compliance
Lightning Source LLC
Chambersburg PA
CBHW030728180526

45157CB00008BA/3087